Turn Me to *Gold*

When you enter into a Kabir poem,
you enter the Kabir field—it is electric,
incisive, clean, and clear. If the sword of
truth could sing, it would sing like Kabir.

—*Andrew Harvey*

Praise for *Turn Me to Gold*

What is it about Kabir? Along with Rumi, he is a mystical poet whose works spring from—and most incredibly, directly invoke in us—the very deepest dimensions of the spiritually drenched human heart. When all is going horribly and you want a powerful reminder of the purest divinity of your own true soul, read Kabir, and celebrate with him the gorgeous wonder and final mystery of existence itself. Andrew Harvey has poured his own heart into a new translation of Kabir, and the result is pure gold. Read this, rejoice with this, share this, be redeemed.

—Ken Wilber, author of *The Religion of Tomorrow*

What a treasure! Andrew Harvey's lush and lucid translations open a fresh window onto the timeless landscape of this beloved mystic. Kabir, like Harvey himself, deftly wove the majestic clarity of Islam with the devotional fire of Hinduism and catapulted beyond both religious spheres to a realm both exalted and grounded. This collection is truly alchemical: the lead of language unfolds into the gold of awakening.

—Mirabai Starr, translator of John of the Cross and Teresa of Avila; author of *God of Love: A Guide to the Heart of Judaism, Christianity, and Islam* and *Caravan of No Despair: A Memoir of Loss and Transformation*

Like water mingling with water, Andrew Harvey mixes with Kabir and finds a new dance, new music, for all of us.

—Coleman Barks, author of *Rumi: The Big Red Book, The Great Masterpiece Celebrating Mystical Love and Friendship*

Wondrous and profound. Andrew Harvey stands alone in his brilliance as a modern interpreter of timeless wisdom. These ecstatic re-creations of Kabir's essential poetry have the spiritual power to transport the reader directly into the Divine presence. More than a literary tour de force, *Turn Me to Gold* is an initiation into mystic awareness that will stay with you for the rest of your life. If you're interested in glimpsing the face of God, buy this book.

—Mark Matousek, author of *Sex Death Enlightenment: A True Story* and *Ethical Wisdom: What Makes Us Good?*

With the arrival of these astonishing poems in *Turn Me to Gold: 108 Poems of Kabir,* "love's hurricane has come." These four stunning symphonic movements are mystical warnings, meditations, incantations urging us past language, logic, delusion, and time. These poems are medicine in these terrible times of corrupt ego and lies. Read them, read them again, repeat them, practice them until the ecstasy of unknowing finally arrives.

—Eve Ensler, author of *The Vagina Monologues* and *In the Body of the World*

***Turn Me to Gold* is balm for the soul.** It is a mystical treasure book. Every poem is a jewel. I hope everyone reads this book.

—Caroline Myss, author of *Anatomy of the Spirit* and *Defy Gravity*

There's no more ecstatic combination than Kabir and Andrew Harvey—ecstatic in that it wakes you up, gets your blood flowing, makes your mind make big connections and your heart begin to hope. Thank you, Andrew, for bringing Kabir into the space of now with all the power that only you can bring.

—Marianne Williamson, author of *Tears to Triumph: Spiritual Healing for the Modern Plagues of Anxiety and Depression* and *Illuminata: A Return to Prayer*

Ever since Robert Bly introduced me to Kabir some 40 years ago, I have been a fan eagerly hunting and gathering more Kabir poems and translations to share Kabir with others. Now Andrew Harvey has brought his magic and deep mystical intelligence to choose and translate a very delicious collection of Kabir psalms. We can all rejoice to see this deeply ecumenical soul from 15th-century India shout his wisdom into our hearts in a fashion that, hopefully, cannot be ignored. How deeply humanity needs Kabir, whether we know it or not! Harvey's collection makes the encounter both exciting and timely!

—Matthew Fox, author of *Christian Mystics: 365 readings and Meditations*, *Passion for Creation: Meister Eckhart's Earth-Based Spirituality*, and *Meister Eckhart: A Mystic-Warrior for Our Times*

If ever there was a time for this magnificent offering, it is right now. This book is no accident. It is divinely intended. It brings together two of the greatest mystics of all time—Andrew Harvey and Kabir—at the moment we need them the most. I see them standing in the center of the sacred battleground, book in hand, sharing the wisdom that will liberate us from our blinding bondage. Finally, we can lay down our arms. Finally, we can surrender to the love that sources the all. They say that great achievements take our breath away. This is not actually true. Great achievements bring us back to life. This book does just that—it revives us and readies us for the next stages of our personal and collective evolution. It breathes hope into our dampened and demoralized spirits. Buy this blazing fire of truth and remember.

—Jeff Brown, author of *An Uncommon Bond* and *Grounded Spirituality*

Andrew Harvey is a gem for gifting the world so eloquently with the powerful renderings of the great weaver and mystic Kabir. These poems will speak to you as you feel your connection to the Divine inside daily life. Kabir writes timelessly in lyrical, passionate poems that sweep across the vast range of human emotions, from the depths of sorrow and despair to the heights of wondrous joy and praise. Savor each illuminating page in this book and come to know the true meaning of love.

—Susan Frybort, author of *Open Passages* and *Hope Is a Traveler*

Andrew Harvey's Kabir has a way of coming closer even than Rumi: "I am always already by your side." These are both masterful translations and first-class poems that speak across the centuries to where we are now in no uncertain terms: to our separation from God, our identification with ego, our lostness in illusion, our disconnection from the great natural rhythms of life and the planet. Right from the first poem we have lyricism and wisdom combined in a unique style; and in irradiated language, we have Kabir standing in front of us, his soul singing, a figure of flame and light and a breaker of chains telling us we can't be free until we are free in our minds. More than anyone, Kabir knew what it was to be trapped by religious mindsets and prejudices in the "City of Death." In the awakening is life, only waiting to be with us, imbued with the Divine that takes us home to who we are as authentic and radical loving people. This is a significant literary as well as spiritual achievement by one of the true teachers of our time who understands the role of the poet as a catalyst for change as well as self-knowledge.

—Jay Ramsay, coauthor with Andrew Harvey of *Diamond Cutters: Visionary Poets in America, Britain and Oceania*

To render Kabir into English, or simply to read him as he stands—to follow the changes and textures of his love—one must have a palate for both the sublime and the earthly, for the taste of honey and also the taste of salt. Andrew Harvey's translations encompass the whole spectrum of Kabir's dance steps under the invisible blows of the Friend, and do so confidently, clearly, and directly—all the kisses, the slaps, the seductive glances, and the sly, quizzical sleights-of-hand, designed to purify love of questions. Form is an open doorway; forgetting this, we invent doors, and then beat our heads (and other people's heads) against them—never more so than today. Kabir came to remind us that the space of the house, the space of the doorway, and the space of the universe are one continuous open field, the taste of which is an indescribable bliss. Kabir came up to Andrew Harvey and said, "Bring me forward again." And so, this book.

—Charles Upton, author of *The System of Antichrist: Truth and Falsehood in Postmodernism and the New Age*

These poems are, in a word, stunning. My mouth drops open in amazement as I read. These verses capture in elegant language not only the essence of the great master /poet/mystic Kabir, but the reality of the human journey into the realm of the "other," the divine unspeakable essence of the deep spiritual path. Andrew Harvey has indeed produced a masterpiece, and who but he is better equipped to lead us on this venture, for he himself is one of the great mystics/wisdom teachers of our time. In an era of chaos and confusion, Kabir, as transmitted by Andrew, offers balm for our souls and refuge from the intrusions of a misguided age. These sublime poems will be read and treasured as long as our world exists and will ever remain as a bold testament to Kabir and his inspired and supremely gifted translator of verses that speak forcefully to our time.

—Dorothy Walters, Ph.D., author of *Some Kiss We Want: Poems Selected and New* and *Unmasking the Rose: A Memoir of a Kundalini Awakening*

Reading Andrew's translations of Kabir is like standing under a waterfall and feeling a surge of joy and deep love for all life. Kabir is a portal to the Eternal and Andrew is a doorway to Kabir.

—Jim Garrison, Ph.D., president, Ubiquity University

Kabir is, for me, the supreme voice of the embodied divine human. Give your all to live these astounding poems if you long to embody your soul. No one transmits Kabir's holy passion as Andrew does.

—Banafsheh Sayyad, dancer, choreographer, founder, Dance of Oneness®

Andrew has written most magnificent poems on Kabir that truly turn our vision to what is truly gold in life. These poems are exquisite prayers of the soul that invite the Sacred to fill our consciousness. I recommend everyone to read them again and again delighting in their beauty and their message of most powerful awakening.

—Chris Saade, philosophical teacher and author of *Second Wave Spirituality*

Andrew Harvey's *Turn Me to Gold: 108 Poems of Kabir* is a sublime meditation on the Great Divine Mystery, an ecstatic celebration of life, love, and joy—an essential antidote to the troubled illusions of our times.

—Brad Laughlin, author of *The Marriage of Spirit: Enlightened Living in Today's World*

This book is an ecstatic bonfire of love!

—Stephen Dinan, president and CEO, The Shift Network

Kabir's time has come in the West. His ecstatic devotional poems of love and passion for the divine invigorate the heart, feed the soul, and nourish the spirit. Like Rumi he speaks with an eternal voice to every human being and belongs to our most precious spiritual and poetic universal treasures. Kabir, as each great poet, needs to be rebirthed for every new generation, his message reactivated, rephrased in the common language of the times. This 15th-century mystic has found the perfect communicator in Andrew Harvey, who, like Kabir, dedicates his life to lead us again to a communion with the Divine. Beyond rigid theories and dogmatic beliefs Kabir offers us an antidote, a medicine, against the cynicism, the materialism, and the narcissism so prevalent in our times.

—Ludwig Max Fischer, Ph.D., translator of Herman Hesse, coauthor of *The Seasons of Soul: The Poetic Guidance and Spiritual Wisdom of Herman Hesse*

The wisdom of the 15th-century mystic Indian poet Kabir remains essential for transforming the challenges we face today in order to manifest a new humanity for people, planet, and all sentient beings. Andrew Harvey's selection and sequence of Kabir's poems brilliantly moves us through an inspiring journey of unfolding our innate compassionate self in order to transcend divisive social forces. Kabir invites us to look within to see our true freedom and unifying power through divine love—a love that is way beyond caste, tradition, and rituals. This book is a must-read for those who want to transform our abundant yet aching world and create universal prosperity for everyone.

—Dr. Monica Sharma, author of *Radical Transformational Leadership: Strategic Action for Change Agents*

Only Andrew Harvey with his mastery of language and passionate poet's heart could have honored Kabir with this sublime rendering of his words.

—Anne Baring, author of *The Dream of the Cosmos: A Quest for the Soul*

This could be quite simply the best poetry book ever written.

—Gabriella Martinelli, owner, Capri Films

If your heart is normal size right now, buy this book. Why? Because this book will expand your heart so wide, so deep, that nothing will be beyond you. Andrew has brought us Kabir with an elegance and grace not found in normal life. He understands greatness and offers it to you here.

—Dr. Scilla Elworthy, author of *The Business Plan for Peace: Building a World Without War*

These exquisite writings serve as a sacred gateway! Every carefully chosen word captures the essence of Kabir, and beckons to us with mystery and delight. Each passionate phrase reveals the invitation of divine connectedness, so secretly tucked in, between the lines.

—Rasha, author of *Oneness*

The poetry of the "divine Kabir" comes alive in these poems—phrases leap from the page, disarmingly vivid, immediate, and fragrant. Translating sacred texts is a high art. Literal scholarly translation falls short because it fails to convey the awakened spirit of the original. Luckily we have Andrew Harvey, an eloquent genius with direct mystical experience and intuitive understanding of the freedom, ecstasy, and union that uttered Kabir's holy words. And luckily, Andrew stays humble and devotionally faithful, intending only to be of generous service to the divine Kabir and his contemporary reader. That's why these translations convey an intuition of the radically illuminated mind that authored them. Thank you for this precious gem!

—Terry Patten, author of *A New Republic of the Heart* and *Integral Life Practice*

The origin of the title *Turn Me to Gold* is a statement by Kabir that one drop of divine love can turn you to gold. What Andrew and Kabir mean by "gold" is someone who is fully embodied—not just inspired in the mind but who experiences God in the body, in the cells. The birth that is trying to take place on our planet is not one of people just becoming conscious of the Divine but who have *integrated* and *embodied* the Divine. Kabir then is the supreme guide for allowing ourselves to be "turned to gold." I invite everyone to read this book and become the gold.

—Carolyn Baker, coauthor with Andrew Harvey of *Savage Grace* and *Return to Joy* and author of *Collapsing Consciously: Transformative Truths for Turbulent Times*

Kabir is one of humanity's most sublime and passionate universal mystics. To read him is to enter into ecstatic communion with the Divine. Andrew Harvey's translations make him available in a holy and powerful way that will inspire all seekers on all paths.

—Gloria Vanderbilt

Andrew Harvey is a great original, an ecstatic, and lover of God, a formidable scholar and writer capable of the most exquisite renderings of other God-mad men. Here, in his translation of these divine and devastating poems, he reveals the depths of who and what he is—the soul mate of Kabir. Read these poems and you will live again.

—Jean Houston

Turn Me to Gold

108 Poems of Kabir

Translations by Andrew Harvey
Photographs by Brett Hurd

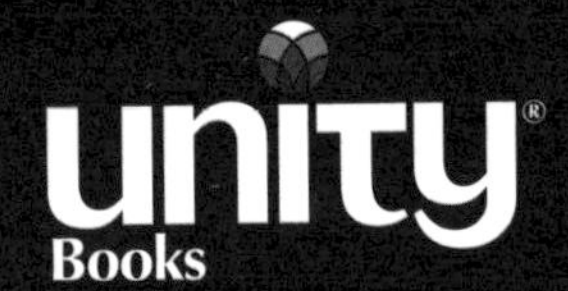

Turn Me to Gold

First Edition 2018

Unity Books are available at special discounts for bulk purchases for study groups, book clubs, sale promotions, book signings, or fund-raising. To place an order, call the Unity Customer Care Department at 816-251-3571 or email *ccwholesale@unityonline.org*.

Cover design by: Kyle Stephan

Interior design by: Hailee Pavey

To create this magnificent pioneering book and layout, some of the photos required cropping. Full renderings of selected photos can be found at *andrewharvey.net* and *bretthurdphoto.com*.

ISBN: 978-0-87159-381-8

LLC Number: 2018944724

Canada BN 13252 0933 RT

Dedication

To all lovers of God and seekers of Truth

Foreword

It has been a supreme honor of my life to have spent five years of it in the secret, unremitting presence of Kabir. What he has given me is beyond any of my words to express because he has come into me and blessed and scourged and broken me and begun to awaken me. What work or thanks of mine could ever be enough for such a gift beyond price?

For five years I have worked with my whole mind, heart, and body on breathing and living his words, the fierce temperature of his truth. I worked, with my smattering of Hindi, with many scholars in India and Europe and from many translations in different languages—French, Italian, German. The ones that have taught and honed me the most are by two amazing women scholars, Charlotte Vaudeville and Linda Hess. I salute them.

All this strange, precise, ecstatic work took place on different continents in the gaps of the busiest and most exhausting period of my life. So I lived with Kabir in airports and hotels and planes and restaurants and trains, walking his streets of Benares (now Varanasi), speaking him to the blazing stones of the Namib desert, dreaming of his ecstatic singing one Christmas in Istanbul. I lost myself deliberately and with awe in Kabir and the limitless life our love was unveiling in me.

This book, *Turn Me to Gold,* is the child of living with Kabir and trying to die into the splendor he sings so it could sing out again its prophecy of divine embodiment.

Kabir is far more than a poet; he is a universal initiatory field, as expansive as Rumi and as embodied, radical, and ferocious as Jesus. He is the voice of the evolutionary truth and its piercing love, and we have never needed to hear him more or been more ready to hear him.

Turn Me to Gold is arranged as a mystical symphony in four movements. Kabir sang his poems in the noisy and filthy alleys of 15th-century Benares; he knew God as the supreme musician whose sound always rang in his ears. Only a rich musical form I knew could ever begin to do justice to the different dancing facets of Kabir's genius and their endless interplay.

In the first movement, "I Am Always by Your Side," Kabir drags us nakedly headlong into his revelations of the direct connection with the One. In the second movement, "True Loves Never Die," these revelations become personal, fierce, alchemical, poignant as a great struggle to die into life starts and surges. The third movement, "Nothing Left to Know," works with both the light and the dark of the One with increasing subtlety to unveil a mystery of union beyond all opposites. The fourth movement, "Each Taste Brings Bliss," is a marriage feast of embodied divine awakening flooded with bliss and peace and gratitude.

May *Turn Me to Gold* be far more than a book to you, as it has been far more than a book to me. Let Kabir guide you, take his hand, let him lead you into the abyss of unknowing where you will find yourself, despite yourself, being turned to gold. All awe and gratitude to Kabir and to you, lovers of truth, who will also find him.

This foreword is dedicated to my great friends Jenny D'Angelo and Jill Angelo Birnbaum. Without Jenny's exquisite editing and companionship, *Turn Me to Gold* would not be what it is. Without Jill's tireless championship of the project and her belief in it, Kabir's voice would not be sounding so strongly. I bow to them both.

Andrew Harvey
Oak Park, Illinois
October 2018

Movement One

I Am Already by Your Side

There is a bird on this body tree
That dances in the ecstasy of life.
No one knows where it is,
And who could ever know
What its music means?
It nests where branches cast deep shadow;
It comes in the dusk and flies away at dawn
And never says a word of what it intends.

No one can tell me anything
About this bird that sings in my blood.
It isn't colored or colorless;
It doesn't have a form or outline;
It sits always in the shadow of love.
It lives within the Unreachable, the Boundless, the Eternal
And no one can tell when it comes or when it goes.

Kabir says, "Fellow seeker,
The mystery of this bird
Is marvelous and profound.
Be wise; struggle to know
Where this bird comes to rest."

Wherever you go looking for Me
I'm already always by your side
I'm not in sacred places
I'm not in temple idols
I'm not in solitary retreats
I'm already always by your side.

I'm not in temples or mosques
I'm not in the Kaaba, not in Kailash
I'm already always by your side.

I'm not in austerities, not in meditation,
Not in feasts, not in fasts
Not in rituals laid down in sacred texts
Not in yogic exercises—

Look for Me with passionate sincerity
I'll be beside you immediately.
Kabir says: seeker, listen to Me—
Where your deepest faith is, I am.

I meditate
On the One only
On the Signless One.
I have no other friend.

No grief comes near me.
No suffering attacks me.
I call no doctor.
Mine is the true teacher
The eternal teacher
Only He can take my pulse.

I don't go down to sacred rivers
I don't bathe in the holy water
The sixty-eight holy places
Are all here, right here,
In my own body
And here, right here
I wash away
Every dark stain.

I don't pluck leaves.
I don't worship stones.
I don't haunt temples.
I don't chop down trees.
I don't grab at shrubs.

I keep mixing
Light with light.
Under the dais
Of the one true teacher
Coming and going are gone.

Between the posts of "conscious" and "unconscious"
The mind has strung a swing;
On it hangs all beings, all worlds
And it never stops swaying.

Millions of beings sit on it
And the sun and moon also,
Millions of eras come and go
But the swing remains.

Everything swings!
Sky and earth, air and water
And the Beloved Himself
As He comes into form—

Seeing this
Has made Kabir a servant.

All creatures are like you—
Allah-Ram.
Be kind to them.

Why beat your shaved head
On the Earth?
Why dunk your bones
In the river?
Doing your "holy" act
You hide yourself
And go on killing.

Why rinse mouth and hands?
Why chant and chant
With a heart full of fraud?
Why keep on bowing in the mosque
Or slog to Mecca
To gawk at God?

Hindus fast for twenty-four days
Muslims for thirty—
One month only for fasting
The other eleven for illusion.

Does Allah live in Mosques?
Who then lives everywhere?
Is Ram only in idols
Or "Holy Ground"?
Did you look and find him there?
Hari in the east, Allah in the west—
Just your fantasy, friends.

(CONTINUES)

All creatures

are like you

Look into your heart
It's there that
Ram-and-Allah live.
Are the Vedas untrue
Or the Koran?
What's untrue
Is your darkened view.
He's one, and one in everyone—
How did you make Him two?

Every man, every woman
Who's ever been born
Kabir says
Is one of His forms.
I'm Ram-and-Allah's silly baby.
He's my "guru" He's my "pir."

Lord, a fire's blazing
Without any fuel.
No-one knows
How to put it out.
I know it spreads from You
Burning the whole world.
Even in water
The flames erupt.
Not one but nine streams burn.
No-one has protection.
As the city burns down
The watchman sleeps smugly
Thinking, "My house is safe.
Let the city blaze
So long as my things are saved."
How can anyone's desires be slaked
In a hunchback's arms?
You think on this, you say,
But stagger from birth to birth
Your body forever unfulfilled.
No-one is as stupid
As the one who knows this
And pretends not to.
Kabir asks: what way out
Could there be for such a fool?

The Lord Himself
Is a guest in your heart—
Why are you still
So desperately seeking Him?
Offer your whole heart to Him
Before night darkens it.
How many eons you've waited
For this momentous chance.
Go near, now, to His heart.
Offer yourself selflessly.
He'll give you
An ocean of ecstasy
And explain to you Himself
Love's mysteries and essence.

Kabir says:
How could I ever express
How blessed I am
To have won
His unshakeable love!

Lord and swan
Are in essence the same:
Just its body
Makes one swan
Different from others.

From the same clay
The potter conjures
Multiple things
In many colors
And innumerable forms.

Milk ten cows
Of different colors
Their milk
Will be the same.

Kabir says:
Abandon your religion
And know that the One,
The Lord of all worlds,
Fills every vessel.

Only its body
Makes a swan different
From other swans:
Lord and swan
Are the same in essence.

I know my Beloved is near
For when He wakes, I wake,
And when He sleeps, I sleep.
Anyone who makes Him suffer
Will be destroyed at the root.
I live wherever lovers sing His praise:
When He moves, I walk before Him
My heart in flames at His beauty.
The endless journey ends at His feet:
Millions of lovers sit there in rapture.
It's the Beloved Himself, my friend,
Who unveils here this story of true love.

Friends, let me try
And tell you
What happened—
Although I can't—
When my Lord
Hurled his spear
Into my heart
He wounded me
And vision erupted
In the middle
Of my body
And syllables
Burst into light.

What is always soaring Free
From any dogma, any concept,
Cannot itself be realized
By anyone who's not also free.

Hunger for the fruits of action:
You'll end up the slave of bondage.
The one who says God's Name
Day and night, night and day,
Will come to know with God's Knowledge,
See with God's eyes, live in God's freedom.

185

My swan, let us fly to that land
Where your Beloved lives forever.

That land has an up-ended well
Whose mouth, narrow as a thread,
The married soul draws water from
Without a rope or pitcher.

My swan, let us fly to that land
Where your Beloved lives forever.

Clouds never cluster there,
Yet it goes on and on raining.
Don't keep squatting outside in the yard—
Come in! Get drenched without a body!

My swan, let us fly to that land
Where your Beloved lives forever.

That land is always soaked in moonlight;
Darkness can never come near it.
It is flooded always with the dazzle
Of not one, but a million suns.

My swan, let us fly to that land
Where your Beloved lives forever.

Kabir says: my mind's grown pure
Pure as Ganges water
Now God's running after me
Calling, "Kabir! O Kabir!"

At the table of lovers
I'm throwing a party
Where everyone's drunk already
On a wine beyond illusion.

Kabir is drunk
On God's Name—
Not from wine
Not from drugs;
Drink deeply
From the cup
Of the Name
And you'll be truly
A God-drunk one.

Kabir is drunk on

God's Name

Who could ever know
The secret of the Weaver?
He spread the Universe
As His warp
Fixed Earth and Sky as pillars
Used Sun and Moon as shuttles
Then He took thousands of Stars
And made the cloth perfect.

He goes on and on weaving
To what end? No-one knows.

Kabir says:
Whether with good string
Or strong dye darkened by karma
The Weaver weaves sublimely.

Who can describe God's form?
Who was there who saw Him?
Neither Vedas nor Koran were there.

Who can define God's "Caste"?
Who can tell God's Secret?
In the God-State
There are no clusters of Stars,
No Sun, no Moon.
No-one is born there
From a Father's Sperm.
There is no world there, no land, no air.

Who can even name that state?
No-one even exists in it
To issue orders or frame laws.
In that state
There's neither day nor night.
So tell me friends,
What family does God belong to?
What Caste could be God's?

"You are That" is the teaching
Of all Non-Dualists,
The message of the Upanishads.
On this rock is built the faith
Of all those who know.
Scholars will tell you the same thing.

(CONTINUES)

Supreme Truth is its own Proof.
Don't all the ones
Who have been liberated
Acknowledge and proclaim this?

Listen, friends,
You'll never be free
So long as you cling
To Caste or Tradition.

The highest cannot be described
And cannot be seen
But it can be lived.
Why give your life
For anything less?

The terror of death
That flays humanity
Doesn't come near me;
I'm not battered
By "sin" or "virtue."
I don't know anything
About "heaven" or "hell."
Kabir says: Listen up, seekers,
Sit nobly on the seat you are.

Unshadowed God is other
Total other.
This expanding creation—
Just eye-shadow.

The Om-sound, the universe—eye-shadow
The vast stretch of space—eye-shadow
Brahma, Shiva, Indra—eye-shadow
Krishna and his Gopis—eye-shadow

Poetry—eye-shadow, the Vedas—eye-shadow
All your refined distinctions—eye-shadow
Science, story, recitation—eye-shadow
All your fatuous facts—eye-shadow.

Eye-shadow nature, eye-shadow Gods,
Eye-shadow worshippers, rituals,
Eye-shadow dancing and singing,
Eye-shadow flaunting your "categories."

How far does all this eye-shadow go?
As far as ascesis, as far as pilgrimage,
As far, even, as "good works."
Kabir says: only very few
Wake up to drop
Eye-shadow and touch

Unshadowed God.

The country I live in
Is a country without grief.
I cry aloud
To king and beggar
Emperor and naked wanderer—
If you're hungry for refuge in Him
Come and settle here with me.
Let all those the world has wearied
Lay down their burdens here.

Come here, my brother, live with me:
You'll cross to the other shore serenely.
My country has no Earth, no Sky,
No Sun or Moon or Stars:
Here, only Truth's radiance blazes.

Kabir says: listen, brother,
Nothing is essential except Truth.

The world's ablaze
In illusion and desire.
The trap of Maya
Is terrifyingly strong.
Only the being
Who has won
The sword of discernment
Can hack himself free.
Take the Name of God, my friend,
As the boat to cross
This brutal ocean.
Without it, you'll never reach
The other shore.
Attaining the Name
Is rare and hard
But I have no need
For any other power.
From beginning to end
And age to age
The Name of God binds me
Directly to God.

I'm mad.
God has made me mad.

You are mad
If you don't know
Your true self.
If you know your self
You would have known the One.

If you don't go mad
In divine love
You'll never know Him.

Kabir says: I am soaked through
With the glorious gold
Of God's love.

As long as you're still a slave
To even the subtlest greed
Or most hidden lust for power
Illusion has its noose
Around your neck
Pulling it every day
Tighter, tighter.

That person who's kind
Who practices righteousness
Who remains at peace
In the world's madness
Who feels all sentient beings
As his or her own self—

This person attains
The Deathless One
And is accompanied always
By the true God.

I've burned my house down;
I'm standing
With a flaming torch
In my hand.
I'll burn yours down too
If you join me
On my march home.

Baffled, choosing for or against,
The whole world gets lost;
Choiceless, rejoicing in Him
That's the true knower.

People are bound together
Donkey tied to donkey.
The one with inner vision
Is the only true person.

Those who walk alone
Alone find truth.
The heart dissolved in love
Never returns again.

Wholeness is complete vision:
Everything is sacred.
Kabir says: this can't be understood
And can never be written.

I am God's assassin
And I'm waiting for you
In the dark alley
Of abandoned love
For when you're brave enough
To run onto my knife.

Conquer the mind
Hack it to the ground
Destroy the evil ego.
Your murdered mind
Will cry, “Beloved! Beloved”
And death will not dare
Touch the tiniest hair
Of your head.

Traveler
You've arrived
At the ocean of joy:
Don't go away thirsty!

Be careful!
Death destroys hope!
A stream of sweet water
Runs close at hand—
Drink from there!
Abandon all thirst
For mirage-water.
Drink and keep drinking
From love's pure spring!

Lovers of God
Drink love's nectar
So love of God
Lives always in them.

Kabir says:
Be one of those
Who drowns desire and fear
In sober steady bliss.

Kabir drank in avidly
The nectar of God's love:
The well-baked pot
Will never again
Be turned on the potter's wheel.

The wine of the Beloved's love
Becomes more ravishing
The more you drink it.
But it is hard to buy
For the wine-seller
Demands your head in exchange.

Many throng around
The wine merchant's stall.
He drinks his fill
Who offers his head,
The rest get turned away
Dry and empty.

You are truly drunk
With the Beloved's wine
Whose bliss
Never changes
When you roam
Like a mad elephant
Forgetful of yourself.

The bliss-drunk elephant
Forfeits its usual grass
For the arrow of love
Burns within his heart:
He's chained to the gate of love
And throws dust on his own head.

(CONTINUES)

The drunken one
Is absorbed in one unknown.
He has overcome desire
Soared free of anxiety:
Under the spell of love's wine
He transcends, while in a body,
The stage of liberation.

The lake in which once
Not even a jug could be lowered
The love-mad elephant
Now bathes in with bliss:
The temple has drowned
Along with its spire
Yet the birds go thirsty.

Kabir exhausted
Many yogic alchemies
But found none
Like the Lord's love:
If even one drop
Enters your body
Your whole being

Turns to gold.

Your whole being

turns to gold.

Movement Two

True Lovers Never Die

You are pure, O my God
You are the ocean
Of supreme bliss!
Even sages and prophets
Hunger for refuge in You:
What chance do I have
A poor beggar at Your door?

Lord of truth, You are the river
That flows deep within each heart.
You are an ocean of mercy and bliss,
And yet You have never blessed me
With one look of love:
My life is misery and despair.

False teachers keep inventing
New ways to guide others
Yet have no qualms
About slaughtering animals
And claim to be evolved souls!
They fake their devotion
Don't know true service
Yet keep begging
And hunger for reward.
Dark-hearted they defy You
Calling blessings down on some,
Slashing others with knives.

Seeing how they act, Lord,
Makes me grief-stricken and helpless.
Lord of truth and love
I am Your slave,
Famished for Your peace.
Accept me
You who are the support
Of all beings
Accept me.

This, I've discovered, is true knowledge—
Those who scramble to get into a boat
Sink like a stone midstream
While the shelterless and abandoned
Reach the other shore.
Those who dare to take
The hard, winding, thorny road
Get to town in the end;
Those who stroll the easy highway
Get robbed or even killed
Soon after they set out.

Everyone's wound in illusion's web—
The so-called "holy" as much as the worldly
And those who run for safety
Under the comforting dais
Of form and ritual and dogma—
Well, life's hurricane lashes them.
Stay out in the open:
You'll be left safe and dry.
The ones Love never savages
Live in boredom and pain;
Those Love devours like a cannibal
Live in bliss forever.
The ones who lose their own eyes
Come to see the whole Creation
Blazing in their own Light;
Those who hold on to their sight
Remain blind as bats in full noon.
When I began to awaken to the Truth
I saw how bizarre and crazy the world really is!

Beloved Lord,
Either I am crazy
Or this world of Yours is.

The very worship You don't care about
Is the one everyone's trapped in—
About the worship You love,
Hardly anyone knows anything.

To love You, love You, and no one else,
That's the worship that delights You.
That is why the soul was parted from You—
To return to You through adoration.

Why get caught in empty formalities?
I sing the glory of my love.
I sing of what I have seen myself.
The one who reaches the rank of Lover
Is the Lord's true worshipper.

(Prostate
Allahabad Bank A/c No.-21044846412, IFSC Code
E-mail : drchandrakant@
Website : www.vaidyasamrat.in/.com
Mo-9452027823
प्रातः 7.00 से 2.00
रजिस्टर्ड डाक्टर बनने के लिए सम्पर्क
का मन्दिर

Night and day I played my life away
With those I believed my friends
And now I am terrified.

The palace of my Lord is set so high
My heart trembles at climbing its stairs,
But I cannot be timid now
If I ever hope to win His love.

My heart must cling to Him.
I must throw off all my veils
And meet Him with my whole body.
My eyes must now perform
The ceremony of the lamps of love.

Kabir says, "Listen, my friend—
He who loves, knows.
If you do not burn with longing
For the Beloved,
Don't bother wrapping your body in rich silk;
Don't bother ringing your eyes with kohl."

Seekers, I've seen both paths.
Hindus and Muslims
Don't want rigor
They love rich food.
The Hindu keeps his fast
Eating chestnuts and milk.
No grain, but no brain either
And he breaks his fast with meat.
As for the Muslim, he prays daily,
Fasts once a year, and goes on
Crying, "God, God!" like a cock.

What heaven could await people
Who slaughter chickens in the dark?
They've abandoned all longing
For kindness or compassion.
Hindus kill with one chop
Muslims let the blood drip
Both houses blaze in the same fire.
Truth has revealed to me
There's no difference between them.
Kabir says: Go beyond religion
Say the Name and rejoin origin.

Has anyone ever died
And come back to tell the story?
This world's enslaved
To illusion and false hope.
Call out to God, my friends,
Call out to God, day and night.
You're gulping the poison
Of worldly desires
And burning away your life
In a ghostly fire.

Why so restless, so impatient, my heart?
He watches over birds, animals, the tiniest insect—
He loved you even when you were in your mother's belly.
Do you seriously imagine
He will not look after you
Now that you are here?

O my heart, how could you bear
To turn from His smile
And stray so far from Him?

You have abandoned your true Beloved
And are hankering after others—
This is why all your works are useless.

Slowly, mind, slowly—
Everything unfolds slowly.
The gardener pours
Hundreds of jars of water:
The fruit arrives
Only in season.

Everyone goes on dying and dying
But no-one dies a true death.
Kabir has met with death
Never to die again.

Everyone goes on dying, dying
Without a second thought.
My death, says Kabir, is an artful death.
The rest die and rot.

You have to die, so die!
All whirlpools come to calm.
The house of love is far away
Know and feel this deeply.

Nothingness dies, the soundless dies.
Even the infinite dies.
True lovers never die.
Kabir says: know this.

The whole world fears death
Death makes my heart ecstatic.
When will I die and give myself
In an ecstasy that never dies?

JAG
PARAG

More than anything else
I cherish at heart
What in this world
Makes me live
A limitless life.

VERY NICE ANAR
रूद्रा
राजू मानकर
9545803890
मानसागरी

O Madman! You've won human birth
And are laying it waste.
How many claimants there are
On your dying body!
Your father and mother
Claim you as their son
And reared you for their own agenda.
Your mistress claims
You're her beloved
And like a tigress
Longs to eat you up.
Wife and children cling to you
For their own selfish reasons
And they want you just as much
As the God of Death wants you.
See that crow and vulture?
They're ogling your death.
Dogs and jackals are circling.

The fire is saying: "I'll burn this body."
The water's saying: "I'll put the fire out
And drown this body in me."
The Earth is saying: "This body
Will dissolve into me."
The air is saying: "I'll scatter
The ashes in all directions."
The house you stupidly call yours
Is a noose tightening round your neck.
You claim your body is yours
But you're feeding it daily
To the furnace of dark desires.
So many claimants, my friend,
Waiting for your body
Yet you suffer your whole life
Struggling to keep it strong.
Madman, you keep claiming, "It's mine."
See this starkly: You are not becoming wise.

You are not becoming

wise.

Hey Brahmins, proud of your caste,
Why weren't you born
Already holding the three staffs?
You're born like an untouchable
You'll die like an untouchable
Yet you flaunt your "sacred" thread
So you can wallow in cash.
If you're really a Brahmin
Born of a Brahmin
Why weren't you born
In a uniquely "Brahmin" way?
And if you're a Muslim
Born of a Muslim
Why weren't you born
Circumcised in the womb?
When you milk two cows
One black, one yellow,
Is there any difference
Between their milk?
You think you're so smart.
Abandon your cunning.
Kabir says: Bow down
Only to the One
Beyond name and form.

Pundit's pedantries
Are all lies.

If saying "Ram"
Bestowed liberation
And saying "candy"
Sweetened your mouth
And saying "water"
Drowned your thirst
And saying "food"
Made your hunger vanish
Everyone would be free.

A parrot gabbles "God"
Like a man
But what can it know
Of the Beloved's glory?
When it flies off
To its jungle
It'll forget the One.
If you aren't seeing and touching
What's the Name worth?

If saying "gold" made you rich
No-one would be poor.

Lovers of delusion and desire
Mock the lovers of God.

Kabir says: worship the One
Or you'll go
Wound in a filthy sheet, to Death City.

The arrow you wounded me with
Yesterday
Has ravished
My heart.
Wound me again, today,
Beloved
With the same arrow
For without it
I am restless and despairing.

Of this body
I'll make a lamp
And of my soul
Burning with longing, a wick;
For oil I'll fill the lamp
With my tears of blood
And by its light I'll see
The face of my Beloved.

In this world's ferocious ocean
I've found a raft,
Bound with the snakes of separation.
If I let go, I'll drown;
If I hold on, I'll be bitten to death.

O human!
Don't kill
Any helpless animal!
Life is equal
In every being.
Nothing can absolve you
Of the sin of killing—
Not listening to teachers
Not reading a thousand Puranas.

The sky's on fire
Raining live coals.
Kabir is burned
And turned to gold
But the world remains
Dead as lead.

Who turns willfully
His face from truth
And loves all that is false—
Save me from his company, Lord,
Even in my dreams.

Only rely on what
You get while alive.

Learn while you're alive.
While you're still
In a body
Realize Him.
While you're alive
Attain liberation.

If you didn't shatter
While you're alive
Karma's chains
How can you expect
Salvation after death?

Those who claim, "After death
Your soul melts into God"
Are giving you
False comfort.
Whatever you gain now
Will be with you then
Or you'll just be
Another inmate
In Death's asylum.

The deluded wander around
Searching for God
In far exotic places.
None of this ends their pain
At returning again and again.
Only if you adore the holy
Will the noose of your Karma be cut.

(CONTINUES)

Only rely on
what you get while
alive.

My friend, only rely on what
You get while you're alive.
Know the truth, cling to it.

Realize the inner guru,
Build faith in the true Name.

It's the holy, says Kabir,
Who are my benefactors
And I am their slave.

T.T.
ISI 1786
ISI

Through devotion to Him
I washed away
The dirt of delusion;
The days I spent
Without devotion
Rankle my heart
Like an arrow's broken shaft.

Devotion to the One
Is hard, unsparing,
A path of blazing fire;
Plunge into the flames
You'll pass through safely;
Waver and wait
You'll be scorched.

A path of blazing

fire

This whole world
Is a field of action;
You plow it
To raise a rich crop
But the wild deer
Of attachment
Ruins the harvest
And most return
Empty-handed to the barn.

CONCERT
MUSIC PARTY
SUNIL PRASANNA
ANSUMAM MAHARAJ
KIRSHNA
SHEHNAI
SAROD
DANCE
SANIS KUMAR
FAIYYAZ KHAN
FULTE
SARANGI
HANSRAJ
SAGAR
SITAR
DANCE
MUSIC PARADISE HALL

The self forgets itself
Like a maddened dog
In the hall of mirrors
Barks himself to death—
Like a lion
Gazing into a well
Seeing his reflection
And pouncing on it—
Like an elephant in rut
Jabbing his tusk
Into a crystal rock.
The monkey grabs
His fistful of sweets
And won't let go
And wanders gibbering
From house to house.
Kabir says: You're all
Parrots on poles—
Who snared you?

Without devotion to the Beloved
All your practices are illusion.
Do them zealously, pursue them passionately,
They'll still be in vain, you ignorant dolt.

Your penances are vain,
Your austerities are vain,
What you consider
Your vast knowledge is vain,
And so, without the Lord's Name,
Are your meditations and contemplations.

Your rites, your rituals are vain,
Your adorations are vain,
All your dos and don'ts are vain;
They just plunge you deeper
Into the sea of delusion
And will never help you reach
The shores of bliss and peace.

People hunger for sense pleasures
And rush to satisfy
The palates of their minds;
Teach them Truth, and all they'll do
Is raise doubt after doubt
And revel in useless quarrels.

Kabir the slave is lost
In love of his Beloved;
All delusion gone,
I've given up vain games.

Everyone says they're
Going to "Heaven."
Where this "Heaven" is
I don't know.

They're just ignorant
Of the mystery
Of their one true self,
Yet spin endless stories
To describe this "Heaven."
As long as you long for "Heaven"
Friend, you'll never
Find your home at His lotus feet.

I don't know
Where "Heaven's" fort stands
Or where its moat and ramparts are
And I don't know
Where its gate is either.
Who can I tell this to?
True Heaven is only
In the company of the Holy.

Everyone says they're going to Heaven;
Where this "Heaven" is
I don't know.

Make your own choice, friends.
See Truth while
You're still in a body.
Find your own place.
When you're dead
What house will you have?
O my friend,
You just don't get
Your one true chance.
Don't you see
In the end
No-one belongs to you?
Kabir says: it's brutal
This turning wheel of time.

Do not blame Love for the agony it brings;
Love is the King of all paths,
And the heart not wild with longing
Is already dead, already a burial ground.

Do not blame

Love

Keep saying God's Name.
Death has you by the hair
And you know nothing
Of when death will kill you
Whether at home
Or in a foreign land.

Swan, the pearls are on sale
Poured out on a golden plate.
If you don't know the secret
What can Kabir do?

Easy to give up wealth
Easy to give up sex
But ego, pride, and jealousy
They're hard to discard.

I bring you a cup of Light
Filled with the wine of Truth
And you, my friends, go on drinking
Dirty water from broken drains.

I am the worst of all
And everyone's better than me;
Realize this and you'll be
Kabir's heart-friend.

When will that day dawn, Mother,
When the One I took birth for
Holds me to His heart with deathless love?
I long for the bliss of divine union.
I long to lose my body, mind, and soul
And become one with my husband.

When will that day dawn, Mother?
Husband, fulfill now the longing I have had
Since before the universe was made.
Enter me completely and release me.
In terrible lonely years without You
I yearn and yearn for You.
I spend sleepless nights hunting for You,
Gazing into darkness after You
With unblinking hopeless eyes.

When will that day dawn, Mother?
When will my Lord hold me to His heart?
My empty body, like a hungry tigress,
Devours me whenever I try to sleep.
Listen to your slave's prayer—
Come and put out this blaze of agony
That consumes my soul and body.

When will He hold me to His heart?
When will that day dawn, Mother?
Kabir sings, "If I ever meet You, my Beloved,
I'll cling to you so fiercely You'll melt into me;
I'll sing from inside You songs of union,
World-dissolving songs of Eternal Bliss."

Movement Three

Nothing Left to Know

Read the book that contains
No letters, no ink,
No numbers, no forms;
Play cymbals with no hands
Dance without feet.

See that home beyond all worlds
Suffused with the radiance
That no lamp lights;
Let the floodgates of the Name
So open that you're swept
Into Supreme Being.

How could I ever express the Secret?
If I say He is within me
The entire universe bangs its head in shame,
Yet if I say He is outside me
I know I'm a liar.
He makes the inner world and the outer one;
Conscious, Unconscious—both are His footstools.

He is neither manifest nor hidden;
He is neither revealed, nor unrevealed,
There are no words to describe what He is.

You are That—does That have a name,
A sex, a caste, a tribe, a religion?
Don't cling to anything man-made.
You are That, formless and eternal.

O scholar, how brilliant you are
Reading book after book.
Tell me now: are you Free?
Do you know the Supreme One?
And the village where He lives?
Tell me His name then.
Brahma created the four Vedas
And even he didn't know
The secret of salvation.
He carried on about
Giving alms and doing good deeds
But hadn't a clue
About his own death.
There is one Name, my friends,
Whose depth cannot be sounded.
And in this Name, God's servant Kabir
Has found unfathomable Peace.

Kabir says: where no ant climbs to
And a mustard seed cannot take root
And birth and death have no power
Go there! Go there! Go there!

It's a hard, exhausting fight
The fight of the truth-seeker.
The vow of the truth seeker
Is harder than the warrior's
Warriors fight for a few hours
The truth-seeker's battle
Goes on day and night—
As long as life lasts
It never ends.

I don't pray for
Miraculous powers
Or wealth and fame
But for one grace only;
Keep me in the company
Of your true saints
Day and night, day and night.

Your soul was orphaned
Through separation from God.
The ones who know say
The Vedas are only imitations
Of the one eternal knowledge.
Become self-realized then
And you'll despise imitations.
A juggler doing his tricks
Knows they're false.
A director claps and enjoys
His dazzling deceptions.
God at play in all beings
Is the only real juggler.
Who could ever match Him?

Whatever chance you get
Good or bad, fabulous or lousy,
Make the very best of it.
Pierced by the arrow of God's love
You'll suffer agonies of separation.
Don't run away from that anguish
You'll realize the ocean of bliss.

Wake up, you idiot.
Shake off your long sleep.
Focus within, discover
The rare wish-fulfilling jewel.
You've slept on and on,
Lost countless days to sloth;
Get up right now
So the plundering thieves
Leave empty-handed
From your house.

This is the sign, friend,
That you're awake;
Vedas, Puranas, Koran
Appear to you like poison.

Kabir says:
I'll never sleep again!
I've found God's priceless jewel
Within my own body.

Within this body
There are gardens and fields
The creator is within it
And all seven seas
And rivers of countless stars.

Within this body
Are both the touchstone
And the jewel-tester.
Within this body
Sounds the Eternal continually
Its music always flowing.

Seeker, listen to me;
My Beloved is within.

Who's fooling who, friend?
The formless is in form
Form in the formless—
So why go anywhere?

Say, "He's young forever"
The invisible stays unsaid.
It has no family,
No character, no color,
And yet suffuses every being.

Some say
"He's in each atom and every world."
Others
"He has no beginning or end."

Another says
"Cosmic, atomic—drop this rubbish!"
Kabir says:
"He's God! He's God!"

The Vedas say
"The formless rests beyond form."
With form or not
Forget everything
And see in all His home
Unstained forever
By joy or grief
Revelation day and night.
Covered in light, sleeping on light
Light pillowing your head.

(CONTINUES)

Who's fooling who,

friend?

Kabir says:
Listen, seeker,
The one true master
Is light throughout.

Calling Him 'heavy'
Frightens me.
Calling Him 'light'
Is a lie.
What do I know of Him?
These eyes have never seen Him

The Lord of Death
Turns into Him.
All grief gone
I stretch out in peace.

Enemy turns to friend.
Demons to helpers.
Now, for me, all is blessed.
Knowing Him, silence pours down.

A million knots in the body
Unwind into simple bliss.
A knowing dawns deep in my heart;
Disease no more can touch me.

Mind has turned into deathless mind.
I know now I was living dead.
Kabir says: I am simply joy,
Fearless, and frightening no-one.

GUEST HOUSE
MIKO HOUSE
BUNKEDUP
HOSTEL
20 Mtr.
NY CAFE
Training Centre
YOGA.REIKI.MEDITATION.
Tripura Bhairavi
BHU
SCHOLARS
ADMISSION OPEN

I've filled this body's pot
With shining pure water;
With body, mind,
And my heart's young passion
I drink, and keep drinking
Yet always thirst for more.

My mind turned back
And dived into the ocean
Of truth and bliss
And bathes in ecstasy;
It tries to fathom You
But how
Could it ever?
You are perfect,
Lord of Mercy,
While it is not.

Searching for Him, friend,
Kabir lost himself;
When drop has merged
Into ocean—
Who can find the drop?

Searching and searching
For Him, friend,
Kabir lost himself;
Ocean has merged
Into drop—
Who can find the ocean?

The street of love is narrow.
Two can never fit.
When I was, I wasn't.
Now He is, I'm not.

Sharp as arrows
The savage words
Of the evil—
But the holy
Are not touched by them;
The ocean is never hurt
By bolts of lightning.

ॐ नमः शिवाय

Lord, the Law's
Over my head.
I don't question it.

You're the river
You're the boatman;
Only through You
Can I cross over.

Devote yourself finally
To the Beloved
Whether He's loving
Or whether He's angry.

Your name, Beloved,
Is my only support.
It sustains my life
As water does the lotus.

Kabir's your slave.
Give me life, or give me
Death. Whatever You want,
Lord, whatever You want.

Truth, that astute warrior,
Shot and wounded me
From my feet to my head;
From outside, I seem whole;
Inwardly, I'm torn to shreds.

Truth,

that astute
warrior,
shot and
wounded me

The touchstone of God cannot fail;
The fake never get past it;
Only he will stand the test
Who, alive, knows how to die.

Lord, when liberated
Where would I go?
They say the soul
Goes up to "heaven"—
What is that and where?

If You keep my soul
Separate from Yours
What's Liberation worth?

What I've known Lord,
Is that You dwell
In all being equally.
Please confirm this!

Make clear to me too,
If death and liberation
Are two different unfoldings—
I don't want to be uncertain.

If soul and Supreme Soul are one
Everything's transparent;
I see one Lord in every being
And remain satisfied.

Nothing left to know.
Only the knowledge left.
Bliss, truth, gratitude—
Gone, all gone.

আশ্বিন

In the World of God
Nothing is impossible.
Even you, mad, greedy, slave
Can become a Saint.

In the World of God

nothing is impossible.

You who know me
I too know you.
Worldly and religious restrictions
Mean nothing to us.

Finer than water
Thinner than smoke
Faster than wind
Kabir's friend.

Finer than *water*

One is contained in all
And all contained in one.
Kabir is contained in awareness
Where duality finds no place.

In all bodies, One
Pure and stainless.
Kabir wanders there,
There Kabir stays.

Movement Four

Each Taste Brings Bliss

My Father is the absolute Godhead
My Mother the embodied Godhead
And I am their divine child
Dancing for them both
On their burning dance-floor.

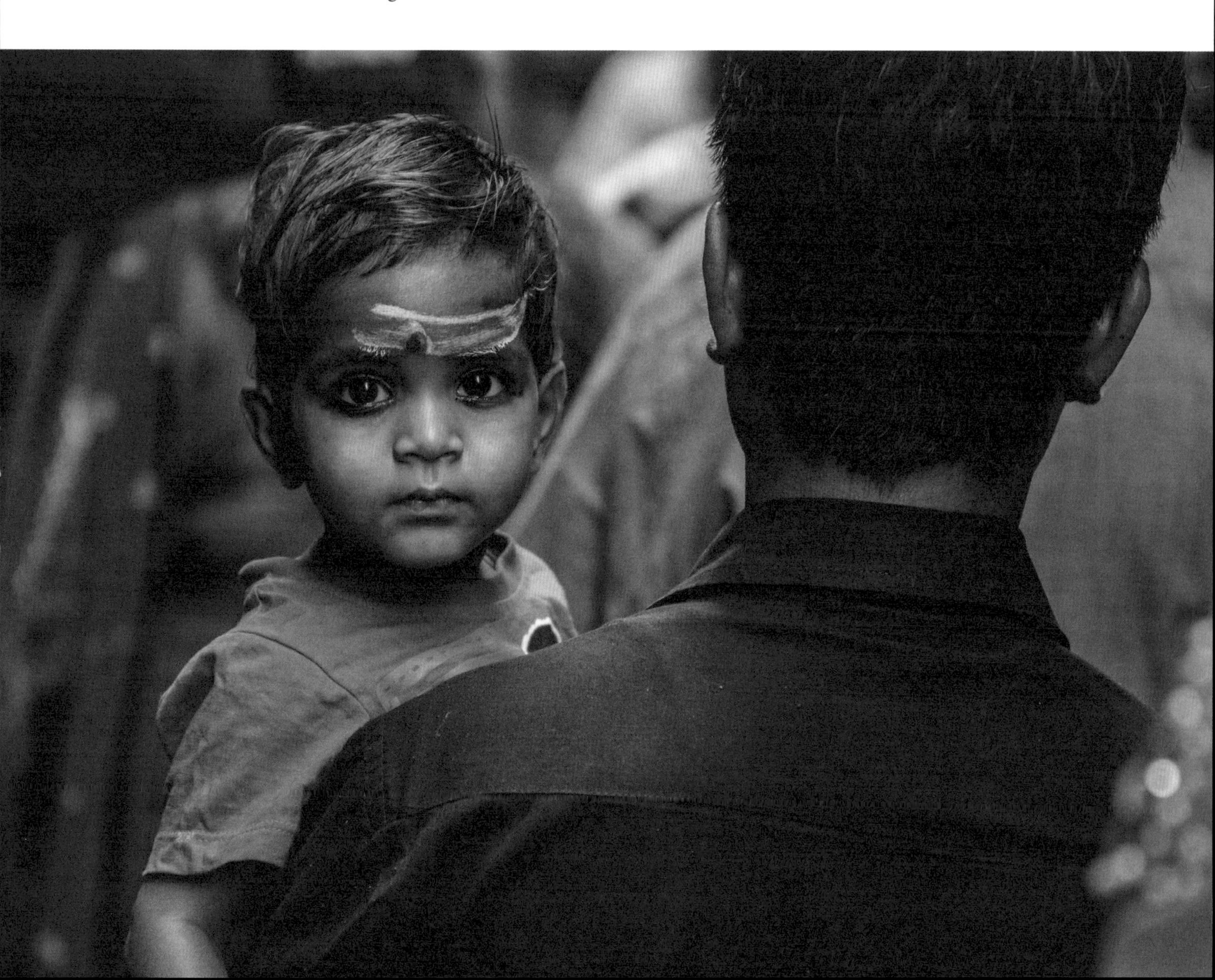

I went looking for Him
And lost myself,
The drop merged with the Sea—
Who can find it now?

Looking and looking for Him
I lost myself;
The Sea merged with the drop—
Who can find it now?

My body is flooded
With the flame of Love.
My soul lives in
A furnace of bliss.

Love's fragrance
Fills my mouth,
And fans through all things
With each outbreath.

In the beginning
No “here” or “there”
No “matter” or “spirit”
Only Love existed.
What was then is now.
This whole universe
Is Love’s endless dance.
Since He showed me this
My heart keeps
Blossoming in bliss.

PRESSURE COOKER
Extra
CELLO
PRESSURE COOKER
शिवा
यू.पी.६२
एफ ७४६५

When the Day came—
The Day I had lived and died for—
The Day that is not in any calendar—
Clouds heavy with love
Showered me with wild abundance.
Inside me, my soul was drenched.
Around me, even the desert grew green.

Even the desert

grew green.

I've found something so rare,
So miraculous,
No-one can assess
How much it is worth.

It is colorless and One;
It is eternal and indivisible;
The waves of change never break over it;
It fills every vessel.

It has no weight; it has no price;
No-one can ever measure it;
No-one can count it;
It cannot be known
Through talk or erudition.
It isn't heavy and it isn't light.
There isn't a touchstone in any world
That can reveal its worth.

I live in it; it lives in me
And we are one, like water
Mingled with water.
The one who knows it
Can never die—
The one who doesn't know it
Dies again and again.

airtel 4G

O holy woman
Sing out the wedding song!
I've come home with Lord Ram
The Beloved of my heart.

Body, mind, all five elements
All loved and offered in welcome.
Ram has come to live with me
And I'm drunk with boundless youth.

My body a pool of Vedas
Brahma himself intones,
United with Ram, round and round,
How blessed I am!

Gods arrive in millions
And sages in thousands.
Kabir says: I'm to marry
And my man's immortal!

The Beloved is in me, and the Beloved is in you,
As life is hidden in every seed.
So rubble your pride, my friend,
And look for Him within you.

When I sit in the heart of His world
A million suns blaze with light.
A burning blue sea spreads across the sky,
Life's turmoil falls quiet,
All the stains of suffering wash away.

Listen to the unstuck bells and drums!
Love is here; plunge into its rapture!
Rains pour down without water;
Rivers are streams of light.

How could I ever express
How blessed I feel
To revel in such vast ecstasy
in my own body?

This is the music
Of soul and soul meeting,
Of the forgetting of all grief.
This is the music
That transcends all coming and going.

Into that music
My mind vanished.
Absorbed in His feet
All grief dissolved.
From the essence-word
A cord, and, on it
The swan rises
And soars free.
On Emptiness Mountain
Cymbals shimmer
Nectar rains down
Drops of love.
Kabir says: seeker, listen—
Here each taste
Brings bliss.

Love's hurricane has come!
The whirlwind of Knowledge has arrived!
My thatched roof of Delusion
Has been flung to the four directions!
My hut of illusion
So carefully crafted
Has come careening down!
Its two posts of duality
Have crashed to the ground!
Its rafters of desire
Have been split by lightning!
Thunderbolts have collapsed
All its eaves of greed!
Its big stone jar of evil habits
Has smashed in a million pieces!

With contemplation and clear devotion,
The Holy Ones have rebuilt my roof.
It is strong and unmoving now
And never leaks or drips.

When lies and deceit
Ran out of my body's house,
I realized the Lord
In all His splendor.
Rain came down in torrents.

After the wild storm,
Torrents of divine love
Drenched me, body and soul.
Then, O Kabir, the sun soared out,
The Sun of Glory, the Sun of Realization,
And darkness dissolved forever.

I’m nobody.
So are you.
What ecstasy!
Join me.

You can't grow love in gardens
Or sell it in markets.
Whether you're a king or peasant
If you want it
Give your head and take it.

Kabir says: clouds of love
Poured down on me
Soaked my heart
Greening my inner jungle.

Aflame, ecstatic
With His Name,
Love—drunk,
Flowing over,
Feasting on
His vision.
Why bother
About liberation?

You can't tell
The story of love.
Not a word of it
Has ever been told.
A dumb man
Eats a sweet
And smiles with joy.

The Lord has made me His
And I am drowned in His love.

Throw this body in the fire
Kabir wouldn't flinch;
Even if I had
To give up my life
I would never break
The bond of His love.

How can love's diamond
Be won for nothing?
I gave up my whole being
And bought the Priceless One.

The One for whom the Gods
Search in vain
I've found within
The cells of my own body.

Kabir says: I've been freed
From the chains of hope and desire;
I have met my Lord
And I am blessed
By faith in Him
That nothing can shake.

The Lord has made me His
And I am drowned in His love.

Seekers, if I speak
Who'll believe me?
If I lie
It passes for truth.
I saw a jewel
Unpierced, beyond price,
Without a buyer or seller.
It flashed, glittering,
In my eyes, and filled
The ten directions.

A touch of grace
From truth, and
The invisible and signless
Appeared. Simple
Meditation, final
Stillness awakened.
Simply, I met Him.
Wherever I look
This only, only this.
The diamond pierced through
My ruby heart.

I have found the one true Name
And It is always with me
Like a string of pearls
Around my neck.
I rest at peace
In the narrow bed
Of the stretcher
Whose five bearers
Are now weak as water.

My master has graced me
The key of keys
To life's unyielding lock;
Whenever I want to
I open the shining door
And dressed in the dancer's robe
Of eternal love
I enter his city
Whenever I please,
And dance in ecstasy.

Kabir says: listen friends,
I will never return
To this city again.

I've understood finally
His magic play.
Beating His drums
He unrolls the show
And rolls it in again.
The Sublime One
Dupes Gods and men and sages.
When He brings out
The witch Maya
She baffles everyone
In every house,
And truth can't get in
To a single heart.
The magic's false
The Magician real—
To the awakened
This is clear.
Kabir says:
What you understand
Is what you are.

Wonder of wonders!
Through action, karma
Came to an end!
In the raging fire of passion
The flower of devotion blossomed
And from this flower
Flames of knowledge leaped out
And ashed all delusion
Of "sin" and "virtue."
The fragrance of adoration
Perfumed my house
And the stink of desire faded.

Knowledge of my origin
Rose in me like dawn;
All thoughts of caste dissolved.
Longing for my true home
Sprang up and consumed
All other cares—
The illusions of the world collapsed.
The Ganges reversed its flow
And raced upwards
To embrace its source.
Earth turned over
And melted into sky.

Kabir, the Lord's truthful slave,
Proclaims: the Moon
Turned back and ate up the Sun.
Wonder of wonders
Through action,
Karma came to an end!

Seeker, the simple union's the best.
Since the day when I met Him
There has been no end
To the joy of our love.
I don't shut my eyes, I don't close my ears,
I don't mortify my body;
I see with open eyes and smile
And see His beauty everywhere.
I say His Name, and whatever I see
It reveals Him: whatever I do
Becomes His worship.
Rising, setting are both one to me;
All contradictions have vanished.

Wherever I go, I move around Him;
Everything I do is service to Him;
When I lie down, I lie prostrate at His feet.

He is the only one I adore; there is no other.
My tongue has abandoned
All impure words and sings
His splendors day and night.
When I get up or sit down
I cannot forget Him;
The pulse of His music
Is always throbbing in my ears.

Kabir says: "My heart is ablaze, I unveil
What is hidden in my soul. I am drowned
In that one great bliss
That transcends all joy and pain."

The Father's beloved son
Ran to try and be with Him;
The Father put
Sweets of greed
In the son's hands—
And faded from the son's mind
As he chewed them down.

When the son
Threw away the sweets
And dared to grow
Deep longing in his heart
With sobs and cries
He followed the Father's path
And came to rest in bliss
In his beloved Father's lap.

Let there be
Your Love, Lord,
Burning softly
In every cell
Of my dying and
Transfigured
Body.

By Your wild
And merciful
Grace, Lord of Truth,
Turn me to Gold

So I can love
In perfect fullness
You
Who Loves in me.

Now I've met my Beloved
My Lord, the emperor of the worlds.
My heart ached for Him
The one whose praise and glory
The Vedas and all scriptures sing—
I've met Him at last, my Beloved, my King.

Pilgrimages and austerities
Can't cut death's noose.
Sins and acts of merit
That cradled births and rebirths
Both are illusions to me now—
Through intense devotion
I've come to meet my King.

Kabir says: I've lit
The flame of knowledge.
I've dived deep, become one
With Love's boundless ocean.
The one I longed for so long
I've met Him, my Beloved, my Lord, my King.

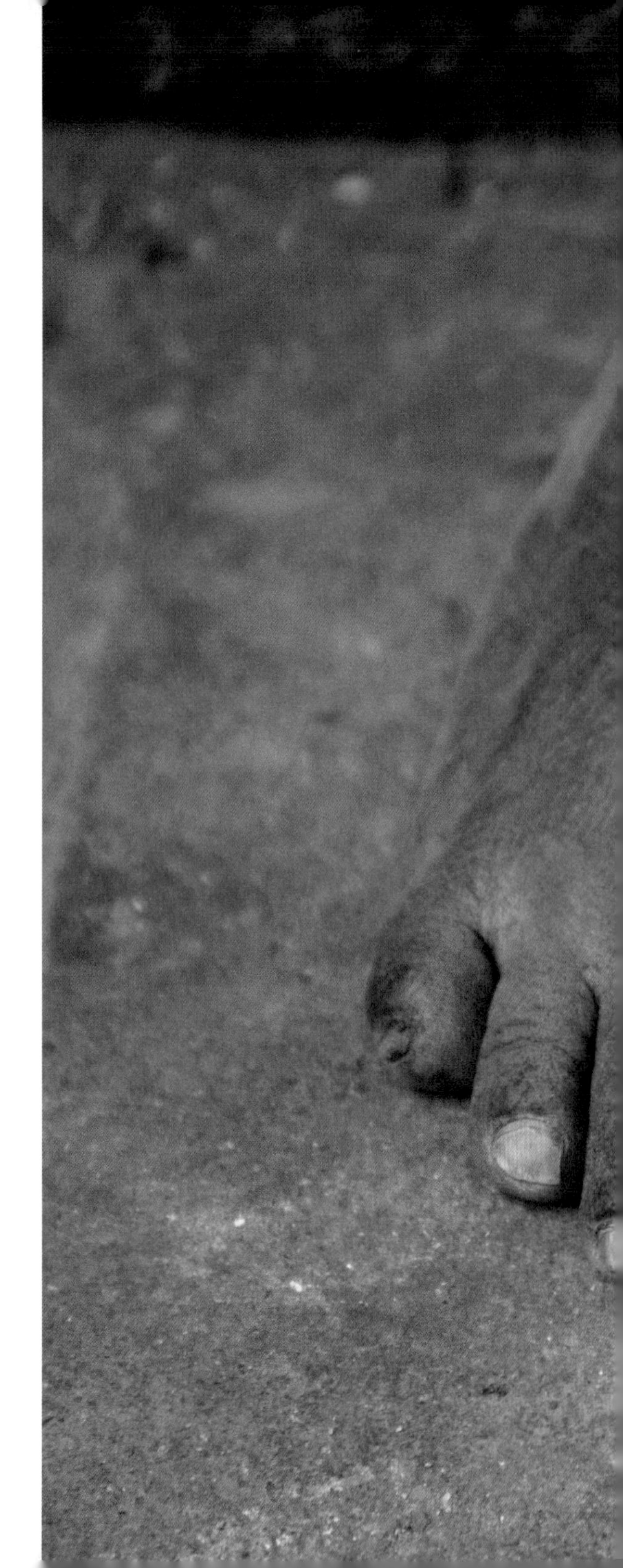

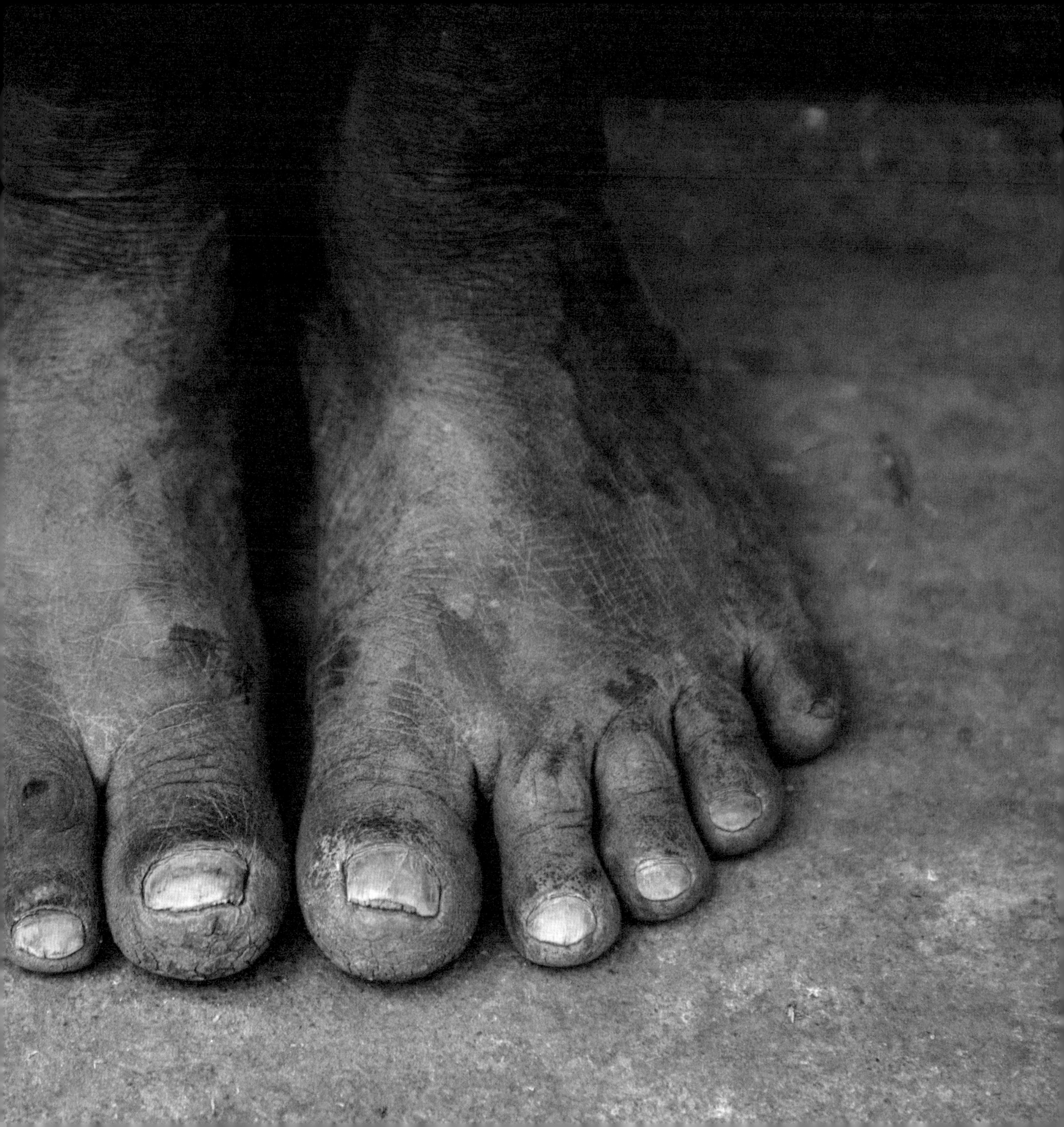

Acknowledgments

To Brett Hurd, for his raw, inspired photographs.
To Ellen Gunter, for her passion for justice.
To Caroline Myss, for her truth.
To Miles Gunter, for his help and friendship.
To Laurel McCullough, for her tireless work.
To Jade, my beloved.
To all at Unity Books, love and gratitude for your integrity and creativity.

Printed in the U.S.A.

B0126